ProMgmt.®

Professional Baking

THIRD EDITION

Student Workbook

National Restaurant Association
EDUCATIONAL FOUNDATION

JOHN WILEY & SONS, INC.
New York • Chichester • Weinheim • Brisbane • Singapore • Toronto

ProMgmt. is a registered trademark of the National Restaurant Association Educational Foundation.

This student workbook is designed to be used with the textbook *Professional Baking, Third Edition* by Wayne Gisslen.

This book is printed on acid-free paper.

Published by John Wiley & Sons, Inc.

Published simultaneously in Canada.

This publication is designed to provide accurate and authoritative information in regard to the subject matter covered. It is sold with the understanding that the publisher is not engaged in rendering professional services. If professional advice or other expert assistance is required, the services of a competent professional person should be sought.

Library of Congress Cataloging-in-Publication Data:

ISBN: 0-471-41302-X

Printed in the United States of America.

10 9 8 7 6 5 4 3 2 1

Contents

Introduction

The professional baker and the foodservice manager face great challenges and reap great rewards from recent changes in public dining. Technological advances in baking and changes in the eating habits of consumers when dining are just two factors that affect the art of professional baking.

Professional Baking, Third Edition will give future foodservice managers and bakers a complete overview of quality baking. The course begins with an introduction to baking, and then looks closely at bread, quick breads, doughnuts, basic sauces, pastries, pies, cookies, custards and fruit desserts, and decoration.

How to Earn a ProMgmt℠ Certificate of Course Completion

To earn a ProMgmt. Certificate of Course Completion, a student must complete all student workbook exercises and receive a passing score on the final examination.

To apply for the ProMgmt. Certificate of Course Completion, complete the student registration form located on the inside back cover of this workbook and give it to your instructor, who will then forward it to the National Restaurant Association Educational Foundation.

Each student registered with the Educational Foundation will receive a student number. Please make a record of it; this number will identify you during your present and future coursework with the Educational Foundation.

ProMgmt. certificate requirements are administered exclusively through colleges and other educational institutions that offer ProMgmt. courses and examinations.

If you are not currently enrolled in a ProMgmt. course and would like to earn a ProMgmt. certificate, please contact your local educational institution to see if they are willing to administer the ProMgmt. certificate requirements for non-enrolled students. You can also visit **www.edfound.org** for a list of ProMgmt. Partner schools. ProMgmt. Partner schools offer seven or more courses that include administration of the ProMgmt. certificate requirements.

The Educational Foundation leaves it to the discretion of each educational institution offering ProMgmt. courses to decide whether or not that institution will administer the ProMgmt. certificate requirements to non-enrolled students. If an institution does administer ProMgmt. certificate requirements to non-enrolled students, that institution may charge an additional fee, of an amount determined by that institution, for the administration of the ProMgmt. certificate requirements.

Course Materials

This course consists of the text, *Professional Baking, Third Edition*, by Wayne Gisslen, the student workbook, and a final examination. The examination is the final section of your course and is sent to an instructor for administration, then returned to the Educational Foundation for grading.

Each lesson consists of:
- Student objectives
- Reading assignment
- Chapter exercises

At the end of the Workbook you will find:
- A study outline of the textbook
- A glossary (when the textbook does not have one)
- An 80-question practice test
- Answers to the practice test

The objectives indicate what you can expect to learn from the course, and are designed to help you organize your studying and concentrate on important topics and explanations. Refer to the objectives frequently to make sure you are meeting them.

The exercises help you check how well you've learned the concepts in each chapter. These will be graded by your instructor.

An 80-question practice test appears at the end of the workbook. All the questions are multiple-choice and have four possible answers. Circle the best answer to each question, as in this example:

Who was the first president of the United States?
- a. Thomas Jefferson.
- (b.) George Washington.
- c. Benjamin Franklin.
- d. John Adams.

Answers to the practice test follow in the workbook so that you may grade your own work.

The Final Exam

All examinations may first be graded by your instructor and then officially graded again by the Educational Foundation. If you do not receive a passing grade on the examination, you may request a retest. A retest fee will be charged for the second examination.

Study Tips

Since you have already demonstrated an interest in furthering your foodservice education by registering for this Educational Foundation course, you know that your next step is study preparation. We have included some specific study pointers that you may find useful.

- Build studying into your routine. If you hold a full-time job, you need to take a realistic approach to studying. Set aside a specific time and place to study, and stick to your routine as closely as possible. Your study area should have room for your course materials and any other necessary study aids. If possible, your area should be away from family traffic.

- Discuss with family members your study goals and your need for a quiet place and private time to work. They may want to help you draw up a study schedule that will be satisfactory to everyone.

- Keep a study log. You can record what lesson was worked on, a list of topics studied, the time you put in, and the dates you sent your exercises to your instructor for grading.

- Work at your own pace, but move ahead steadily. The following tips should help you get the most value from your lessons.

  1. Look over the objectives carefully. They list what you are expected to know for the examination.

  2. Read the chapters carefully, and don't hesitate to mark your text—it will help you later. Mark passages that seem especially important and those that seem difficult, as you may want to reread these later.

3. Try to read an entire chapter at a time. Even though more than one chapter may be assigned in a lesson, you may find you can carefully read only one chapter in a sitting.

4. When you have finished reading the chapter, go back and check the highlights and any notes you have made. These will help you review for the examination.

Reviewing for the Final Exam

When you have completed the final exercise and practice test, you will have several items to use for your examination review. If you have highlighted important points in the textbook, you can review them. If you have made notes in the margins, check them to be sure you have answered any questions that arose when you read the material. Reread certain sections if necessary. Finally, you should go over your exercises.

The ProMgmt. Program

The National Restaurant Association Educational Foundation's ProMgmt. Program is designed to provide foodservice students and professionals with a solid foundation of practical knowledge and information. Each course focuses on a specific management area. For more information on the program, please contact the National Restaurant Association Educational Foundation at 800.765.2122 (312.715.1010 in Chicagoland) or visit our web site at **www.edfound.org**.

Lesson 1

STUDENT OBJECTIVES

After completing this lesson, you should be able to:

- Measure ingredients using U.S. and metric weights.

- Express formulas using baker's percentages.

- Describe how gluten develops through mixing.

- List and describe the steps in the baking process.

- Explain why baked goods become stale and how to slow the staling process.

- List several different types of flours, meals, and starches and describe their different uses in baking.

- List and describe sugars and sweetening agents commonly used in baking.

- List and describe fats commonly used in baking.

- Outline the role of milk and milk products in baking.

- Describe and classify eggs and outline their functions in baking.

- Define leavening and describe leavening agents and how they are used in baking.

- List ingredients used for flavoring bakery products, including fruits and nuts, chocolate and cocoa, salt, spices, and other flavorings.

Reading Assignment

Now read Chapters 1 and 2 in the text. Use this information to answer the questions and activities in Exercises 1 and 2.

Chapter 1 Exercise

1. Which of the following ingredients must always be scaled, and which ingredients can sometimes be measured by volume?

_____ (1) Flour

_____ (2) Shortening

_____ (3) Eggs

_____ (4) Sugar

_____ (5) Milk

_____ (6) Water

_____ (7) Leavening

2. When baking a large batch of bread, should the water be measured by scale or volume? Why?

_____

_____

3. Match each metric prefix with the percentage it represents.

_____ (1) Deci-   a. 1000

_____ (2) Milli-   b. 0.1 (or 1/10)

_____ (3) Centi-   c. 0.01 (or 1/100)

_____ (4) Kilo-   d. 0.001 (or 1/1000)

4. Approximately how many pounds are in a kilogram?

_____

5. A formula calls for 57 percent milk and you are using 3.5 pounds of flour. How many pounds of sugar are needed?

_____

6. If a formula calls for 4 pounds of bread flour, would 4 pounds of cake flour be a suitable substitute? Why or why not?

_____

7. What happens to gluten during each of the following steps?

    (1) Addition of water to flour

    _____

    (2) Mixing and kneading

    _____

    (3) Leavening

    _____

    (4) Baking

    _____

8. What three gases are primarily responsible for leavening baked products?

    • _____

    • _____

    • _____

9. Why is bread best stored at room temperature in the short term?

_____

_____

10. What are four techniques used to slow staling?

    • _____

    • _____

    • _____

    • _____

1. Describe the following flours, and give a use for each.

   (1) Straight flour

   _____

   _____

   (2) Patent flour

   _____

   _____

   (3) Clear flour

   _____

   _____

   (4) Cake flour

   _____

   _____

   (5) Pastry flour

   _____

   _____

2. Match each starch with its primary use.

   _____(1) Cornstarch

   _____(2) Waxy maize

   _____(3) Instant starch

   a. Fruit pie fillings and for products to be frozen

   b. Cream pies and other products that must hold their shape

   c. Fresh fruit glazes and cold liquids

3. What is invert sugar? What are some of its uses in a bake shop?

   _____

   _____

4. Match each sweetener with its definition.

_____(1)   Brown sugar

_____(2)   Molasses

_____(3)   Corn syrup

_____(4)   Honey

a.   Concentrated sugarcane juice

b.   Sucrose combined with varying amounts of caramel, molasses, and other impurities

c.   Liquid sweetener comprised primarily of water, dextrin, and dextrose, made by breaking down cornstarch into simple compounds

d.   Natural sugar syrup comprised of glucose, fructose, and other impurities

5. A uniform mixture of two unmixable ingredients is called a(n)

a.   batter.

b.   simple syrup.

c.   emulsion.

d.   blend.

6. List three functions of fats in baked goods.

- _____

- _____

- _____

7. What happens to liquid oils when they are hydrogenated?

_____

_____

8. What kind of milk can be used when a formula calls for sour milk?

_____

_____

9. What is the optimum storage temperature for shell eggs?

    a.   24°F (−4°C)

    b.   36°F (2°C)

    c.   42°F (6°C)

    d.   65°F to 75°F (18°C to 24°C)

10. In addition to providing nutritional value, flavor, and color to baked goods, eggs perform what functions?

_____

_____

11. Explain how yeast functions to leaven bread and other baked products.

_____

_____

12. Match each chemical leavener with the conditions necessary for its activation.

    _____(1)   Baking soda

    _____(2)   Single-acting baking powder

    _____(3)   Double-acting baking powder

    _____(4)   Baking ammonia

    a.   Requires moisture and an acid

    b.   Requires heat and moisture

    c.   Requires only moisture

    d.   Releases some gases when cold but requires heat for complete activation

13. Of the leavening agents in question 12, which two can be used only if the product is to be baked immediately after mixing?

_____

_____

14. If a formula calls for 2 pounds of bitter chocolate, how much natural cocoa and shortening would be necessary as a substitute?

_____

_____

15. Besides providing flavor, what are two functions of salt in baking?

- _____

- _____

Lesson 2

YEAST DOUGHS

Student Objectives

After completing this lesson, you should be able to:

- Compare yeast product types.

- List and describe the twelve steps in yeast dough production.

- List and describe the three basic dough mixing methods.

- Explain how to control yeast fermentation.

- Discuss the causes of common bread faults.

- Describe the characteristics of different doughs.

Reading Assignment

Now read Chapters 3–5 in the text. Use this information to answer the questions and activities in Exercises 3–5.

Name ——————————————— SS # ———————

Professional Baking, Third Edition Student Workbook

1. Why is a brioche classified as a rich dough product, and a kaiser roll classified as a lean dough product?

   ———————————————————————————————

   ———————————————————————————————

2. How do croissants get their flaky texture?

   ———————————————————————————————

   ———————————————————————————————

3. What essentially is the only step in the straight dough method of mixing yeast products?

   ———————————————————————————————

   ———————————————————————————————

4. In the straight dough method, what ingredient is likely not to be mixed in evenly?

   ———————————————————————————————

5. What are the characteristics of a yeast dough that has been properly mixed? How does overmixing damage dough?

   ———————————————————————————————

   ———————————————————————————————

6. How many ounces of extra dough are necessary to produce one pound of baked bread?

   ———————————————————————————————

   ———————————————————————————————

7. What is the purpose of rounding a piece of dough?

_____

_____

8. What does it mean to bench proof dough?

_____

_____

9. Match the product with its proper baking temperature.

_____(1)   Hard-crusted French bread

_____(2)   Popular American lean bread

_____(3)   Rich products

a.   350°F to 400°F (177°C to 205°C)

b.   400°F to 425°F (205°C to 218°C)

c.   425°F to 475°F (218°C to 246°C)

10. After baking, bread should be allowed to cool inside the pan for two hours. True or false? Explain your answer.

_____

_____

Chapter 4 Exercise

1. What two factors contribute to the crisp, thin crusts of French, Italian, and Vienna breads?

   - _____

   - _____

2. True or false? French and Italian bread doughs have clearly different formulas.

   _____

   _____

3. What two purposes are fulfilled by a sour?

   - _____

   - _____

4. What equipment is used to prepare English muffins and crumpets?

   _____

   _____

5. How are bagels prepared before baking?

   _____

   _____

6. Rolls made from three same-sized dough balls placed in a greased muffin tin are called

   a. Parker House rolls.

   b. cloverleaf rolls.

   c. butterflake rolls.

   d. pan rolls.

7. Why are Pullman loaves useful for making sandwiches?

_____

_____

8. Challah dough contains which of the following?

    a.   Egg yolks

    b.   Egg whites

    c.   Whole eggs

Chapter 5 Exercise

1. Which mixing method is used for most sweet doughs and rich doughs?

_____

_____

2. Why are rich doughs soft?

_____

_____

3. What happens when a rich dough is overproofed?

_____

_____

4. Which require more careful handling, lean doughs or rich doughs?

_____

_____

5. How soon after baking should clear glaze be applied to sweet dough products?

_____

_____

Lesson 3

QUICK BREADS, DOUGHNUTS, BASIC SAUCES, AND PIES

Student Objectives

After completing this lesson, you should be able to:

- Describe the characteristics and mixing methods of quick breads.

- List the different formulas for quick breads.

- List and describe the procedure for doughnuts.

- List and describe the procedure for fritters.

- List and describe the procedures for pancakes, waffles, and crêpes.

- Explain sugar cooking and the role of sugar syrups in baking.

- Discuss the preparation of basic creams, icings, and dessert sauces.

- Compare and contrast the preparation of flaky and mealy pie dough.

- Explain how to assemble, fill, and bake pies.

- Discuss the causes of common pie faults.

Reading Assignment

Now read Chapters 6–9 in the text. Use this information to answer the questions and activities in Exercises 6–9.

Name _____ SS # _____

Professional Baking, Third Edition Student Workbook

1. What are the two types of batters?

   • _____

   • _____

2. Tunneling in muffins is caused by which of the following?

   a.   Undermixing

   b.   Overmixing

   c.   Too little gluten development

   d.   Improper makeup

3. How are popovers leavened?

   _____

   _____

4. What mixing method is used to make scones?

   _____

   _____

5. By how much do biscuits increase during baking?

   _____

   _____

6. Biscuits sometimes are brushed with egg wash or milk during baking. Why?

   _____

   _____

7. How should batter be portioned into muffin tins?

_____

_____

Name	SS #

Professional Baking, Third Edition Student Workbook

1. What mixing method is used to make yeast doughnuts?

_____

_____

2. Why should doughnuts be thoroughly drained and cooled before icing or rolling in sugar?

_____

_____

3. Which is the proper fat temperature range for frying yeast-raised doughnuts?

   a.   190°F to 210°F

   b.   240°F to 260°F

   c.   285°F to 305°F

   d.   365°F to 385°F

4. What is a frying fat's smoke point?

_____

_____

5. Which of the following is made of fried éclair paste?

   a.   Beignet soufflé

   b.   Cannoli

   c.   Fattigman

   d.   Crêpe

6. What three factors distinguish a waffle batter from a pancake batter?

- _____
- _____
- _____

7. Pancake and waffle batter leavened by baking soda may be prepared in advance and stored overnight for use the next day. True or false?

_____

_____

8. What is a gaufre?

_____

_____

1. The process of chemical inversion prevents which of the following?

    a. Burning of crêpes

    b. Crystallization of sugar

    c. Formation of gluten

    d. Breakdown of fats

2. What is the best way to check the hardness of cooked sugar?

    _____

    _____

3. How is simple syrup made?

    _____

    _____

4. Crème chantilly is flavored with what?

    _____

    _____

5. What happens when cream is overwhipped?

    _____

    _____

6. Cream that is slightly old whips better than cream that is very fresh. True or false?

    _____

    _____

7. Two quarts of fresh cream will make approximately how much whipped cream?

_____

_____

8. Why should egg whites for a meringue be free of yolks?

_____

_____

9. Which of the following meringues is most stable?
   a. Italian
   b. Common
   c. Swiss
   d. Swedish

10. Vanilla custard sauce, or crème anglaise, is made from which of the following ingredients?
   a. Eggs, simple syrup, and vanilla
   b. Eggs, sugar, milk, and vanilla
   c. Egg yolks, sugar, milk, and vanilla
   d. Egg whites, sugar, milk, and vanilla

Chapter 9 Exercise

1. What type of flour is best for making pie dough? Why?

———

———

2. What are two reasons pie dough should be kept cool, about 60°F (16°C)?

- ———————————————————————————————————————

- ———————————————————————————————————————

3. Match each pie dough characteristic with the type it describes. Letters will be used more than once.

_____(1) Shortening is rubbed into the flour until particles the size of a pea are formed

_____(2) Has little gluten development

_____(3) Formula calls for more water

_____(4) Used for top crusts

_____(5) Used for bottom crusts because baked dough is less likely to become soggy when filled

   a.   Mealy pie dough

   b.   Flaky pie dough

4. Crumb crusts are used primarily for what kind of pies?

———

———

5. What starch is most commonly used to thicken cream pies?

———

———

6. What thickens custard, pumpkin, and pecan pies?

_____

_____

7. What are two ways to test a custard pie for doneness?

- _____

- _____

Lesson 4

PASTRIES, TARTS, AND CAKES

Student Objectives

After completing this lesson, you should be able to:

- Describe how to prepare pâte brisée, short pastry, puff pastry, pâte à choux, and strudel; and bake meringues.

- Describe how to prepare baked tarts and tartlets.

- Demonstrate basic cake mixing methods including creaming, two-stage, flour batter, sponge, angel food, and chiffon.

- Discuss the concept of balancing cake formulas.

- Explain the processes of scaling, panning, and baking cakes.

- List and describe several different types of icing.

- Explain assembling and icing simple cakes.

- Describe basic cake decorating techniques.

- Explain the planning and assembling of a variety of specialty cakes and cake-based desserts.

Reading Assignment

Now read Chapters 10–14 in the text. Use this information to answer the questions and activities in Exercises 10–14.

Name ——————————————————— SS # ———————————

Professional Baking, Third Edition Student Workbook

1. Describe blitz puff pastry. What is a common use?

——

——

2. What is the preferred fat for puff pastry?

——

——

3. Which of the following are the proper baking temperatures for products made with éclair paste?
   a.   325°F (163°C) for first fifteen minutes; 275°F (135°C) thereafter.
   b.   350°F (177°C) for first fifteen minutes; 300°F (149°C) thereafter.
   c.   400°F (204°C) for first fifteen minutes; 350°F (177°C) thereafter.
   d.   425°F (220°C) for first fifteen minutes; 375°F (190°C) thereafter.

4. Should éclair paste be baked in greased tins? Why or why not?

——

——

5. What are two guidelines that must be followed when handling commercially made phyllo dough?
   • ————————————————————————————————————
   • ————————————————————————————————————

1. Which of the following fruits typically are precooked in syrup or sautéed before being added to a tart?

    a. Cherries

    b. Apples

    c. Strawberries

    d. Pears

2. Generally, what do "French pastries" have in common?

    _____

    _____

3. How do tart pans differ from pie pans?

    _____

    _____

4. What is the primary convenience of using false-bottom tart pans?

    _____

    _____

5. Why should flavorful doughs be used for tarts?

    _____

    _____

Chapter 12 Exercise

1. Match each mixing method with the resulting type of cake. Letters will be used more than once.

   _____(1) Creaming method   a.   High-fat or shortened cakes

   _____(2) Chiffon method   b.   Low-fat or foam-type cakes

   _____(3) Angel food method

   _____(4) Two-stage method

   _____(5) Sponge method

   _____(6) Flour-batter method

2. What happens to the particles in a batter when curdling occurs?

   _____

   _____

3. What are four steps that can be taken to avoid curdling?

   • _____

   • _____

   • _____

   • _____

4. Why is the proper formation of air cells important in a cake batter?

   _____

   _____

5. In the sponge method, creaming method, and angel food method, why is the flour added at or near the end of the mixing process?

   _____

   _____

6. Is it recommended to substitute shortening for butter in equal measure? Why or why not?

_____

_____

7. True or false? High-ratio cakes are so called because they contain a large percentage of liquid.

_____

8. Which of the following characterizes a sponge cake?

   a.   Egg white foam   c.   Egg foam with yolks

   b.   High fat content   d.   Custard

9. When making an angel food cake, egg whites should be whipped to which consistency?

   a.   Until creamy

   b.   Until they form stiff peaks

   c.   Until they form soft peaks

   d.   Until they reach a temperature of 110°F (43°C)

10. What ingredients cause leavening in a chiffon cake?

_____

11. Briefly explain the principles behind formula balancing.

_____

_____

12. When baking cake at an altitude above 2,000 feet the amount of baking powder should be increased. True or false? Explain your answer.

_____

_____

Name	SS #

Professional Baking, Third Edition Student Workbook

1. Which icing provides a shiny, nonsticky coating?

    a.   Foam

    b.   Buttercream

    c.   Royal

    d.   Fondant

2. Why is buttercream best used in cool weather?

    _____

    _____

3. Foam or boiled icing is similar to which of the following?

    a.   Meringue

    b.   Fondant

    c.   Buttercream

    d.   Glaze

4. Which icing is used most often to decorate cakes?

    _____

    _____

5. Match each cake-decorating tool with its description.

_____(1)   Star tip
_____(2)   Sugar dredger
_____(3)   Turntable
_____(4)   Palette knife

   a.   Used for dusting
   b.   Pedestal used for icing
   c.   Used to make rosettes and shell borders
   d.   Used to spread and smooth icings

6. Describe the falling method of decorating cakes.

_____

_____

7. Describe the contact method of decorating cakes.

_____

_____

8. Which are easier to clean, cotton or nylon bags?

_____

_____

1. The German word "torte" refers to which kind of cake?

——

——

2. What are the two key ingredients in marzipan?

• ——

• ——

3. Match each cake with its filling.

_____(1)   Othello

_____(2)   Iago

_____(3)   Desdemona

_____(4)   Rosalind

a.   Rosewater whipped cream

b.   Vanilla whipped cream

c.   Chocolate pastry cream

d.   Coffee pastry cream

4. What are the two types of petits fours?

• ——

• ——

Lesson 5

Student Objectives

After completing this lesson, you should be able to:

- List and describe cookie characteristics and their causes.

- Discuss cookie preparation fundamentals.

- Explain the preparation of custards, puddings, Bavarians, mousses, and soufflés.

- Compare and contrast churn-frozen and still-frozen desserts.

- List and describe traditional fruit desserts.

Reading Assignment

Now read Chapters 15–18 in the text. Use this information to answer the questions and activities in Exercises 15–18.

1. Match each cookie characteristic with one of its causes.

_____(1) Crispness

_____(2) Softness

_____(3) Chewiness

_____(4) Spread

a. High sugar and fat content

b. Baked on a heavily greased pan

c. Contains hygroscopic sugars such as honey, molasses, or corn syrup

d. High sugar and liquid content, low fat content

2. What are the eight methods of cookie makeup?

- _____
- _____
- _____
- _____
- _____
- _____
- _____
- _____

3. Although many bakers used the bagged method for many "dropped" cookies, when is it advisable to use a scoop to drop cookie dough onto the sheet?

_____

_____

4. Which cookie makeup method consists of forming the dough into cylinders, chilling it overnight, slicing the dough into the desired thickness, and baking?

   a. Rolled

   b. Molded

   c. Icebox

   d. Bar

5. When preparing pans for baking cookies, what can be done to eliminate the need to grease the pans?

   _____

   _____

6. How can you tell when a cookie is done?

   _____

   _____

7. Give four examples of petit fours sec. How small must a cookie be to be considered a petit four?

   - _____

   - _____

   - _____

   - _____

   _____

1. What is a custard? Describe the two basic types of custard.

   _____

   _____

2. Which of the following is true of cream pudding?

   a. The formula is essentially the same as that for cream pie filling, but requires only half the starch.

   b. The formula is the same as that for cream pie filling.

   c. The formula is essentially the same as that for cream pie filling but uses twice the amount of starch.

   d. The formula is like a blancmange, because it contains no eggs.

3. How can a cream pudding be prepared using cornstarch pudding as a base?

   _____

   _____

4. List three techniques that improve the quality of baked custards and puddings.

   • _____

   • _____

   • _____

5. What is the procedure for steaming a pudding on top of the stove?

   _____

   _____

6. What is the name of a molded dessert that consists of custard sauce, gelatin, and whipped cream?

   a.   Mousse

   b.   Soufflé

   c.   Bavarian, or Bavarian cream

   d.   Baked Alaska

7. Why must a soufflé be served immediately after being removed from the oven?

   _____

   _____

8. With what is blancmange thickened?

   _____

   _____

9. What are the three main ingredients in a Bavarian cream?

   • _____

   • _____

   • _____

10. What leavens soufflés?

   _____

   _____

1. Match each frozen dessert with its description.

   _____(1)   Philadelphia-style ice cream

   _____(2)   French-style ice cream

   _____(3)   Sorbet

   a.   Smooth, rich ice cream containing egg yolks

   b.   Frozen mixture of fruit juice, water, sugar, and sometimes egg whites

   c.   Ice cream containing no eggs

2. Overrun refers to increase in volume of ice cream as what is incorporated?

   _____

3. Explain why ice cream should be frozen rapidly and churned well during freezing.

   _____

   _____

4. Which of the following terms is synonymous with "coupe?"

   a.   Sundae

   b.   Sherbet

   c.   Bombe

   d.   Gâteau

5. What ingredient characterizes frozen mousses?

   _____

   _____

Chapter 18 Exercise

1. What is a compote?

   _____

   _____

2. Put very simply, what has been the impact of modern technology on fruit consumption?

   _____

   _____

3. True or false? Fall and winter apples keep well, while summer apples do not.

   _____

   _____

4. "Cassis" is another word for which of the following?
   a. Cranberry
   b. Black currant
   c. Raspberry
   d. Lingonberry

5. How large are kumquats?

   _____

   _____

6. Crenshaw, Casaba, and Canary are varieties of which fruit?

   _____

   _____

7. Which of the following fruit desserts resembles a pie without a bottom crust?

    a. Betty
    b. Bombe
    c. Cobbler
    d. Compote

Lesson 6

Student Objectives

After completing this lesson, you should be able to:

- Demonstrate attractive dessert presentations.

- Explain the process and purpose of tempering chocolate.

- Describe the use of chocolate in dessert recipes and as decoration.

- Describe how marzipan, pastillage, and nougatine are made and used as decorations and showpieces.

- Demonstrate techniques for using sugar to make decorations and showpieces.

Reading Assignment

Now read Chapters 19–22 in the text. Use this information to answer the questions and activities in Exercises 19–22.

1. What are the four basic ways to present a dessert?

    • _____

    • _____

    • _____

    • _____

2. List three garnishes suitable for desserts.

    • _____

    • _____

    • _____

3. What are the two standard ways to serve sauce with a dessert?

    • _____

    • _____

4. Elaborate desserts should be served on plates with elaborate designs. True or false?

    _____

    _____

5. Give an example of a dessert presented with matching elements. Give an example of a dessert presented with contrasting elements.

    _____

    _____

    _____

    _____

1. What are the two advantages of coating (baking) chocolate over couverture?

   - _____

   - _____

2. What is the function of lecithin in dark couverture?

   _____

3. What would the numbers 60/40/30 mean on a package of couverture?

   _____

   _____

4. What are the three general steps to tempering?

   - _____

   - _____

   - _____

5. Why must tempered chocolate be rewarmed?

   _____

   _____

6. Describe why chocolate is removed easily from molds.

   _____

   _____

7. Which is thickest: couverture, tempered chocolate, or modeling chocolate?

   _____

8. What is mixed with chocolate to make ganache?

_____

Name _____ SS # _____
Professional Baking, Third Edition Student Workbook

1. Since marzipan is sticky, with what should you dust the working surface and rolling pin?

   _____

   _____

2. Why is pastillage inedible?

   _____

   _____

3. How should unused portions of pastillage be stored while working?

   _____

   _____

4. Why is pastillage an ideal canvas for chocolate painting?

   _____

   _____

5. What nut is a key ingredient in both marzipan and nougatine?

   _____

   _____

1. True or false? When boiling syrup, the higher the temperature, the harder the sugar will be.

   _____

2. Why is it suggested that a beginning chef practice working with syrups boiled at lower temperatures?

   _____

   _____

3. What happens when too much cream of tartar is added to syrup? Why?

   _____

   _____

4. When should cream of tartar be added to boiled syrup? Why?

   _____

   _____

5. Syrup should be boiled
   a.   slowly over low heat.
   b.   slowly over moderate heat.
   c.   rapidly over moderate heat.
   d.   rapidly over high heat.

6. Name at least three measures to take to ensure a quality syrup.

   • _____

   • _____

   • _____

7. True or false? Spun sugar keeps well and can be made up to twenty-four hours in advance.

_____

_____

8. Name at least three tools necessary to pull sugar, and explain their functions.

- _____

- _____

- _____

Study Outline

Chapter 1

1. To obtain the utmost baking accuracy, bakers use a system of weighing or "scaling" ingredients.
   a. Bakers use a baker's balance scale and a system of baker's percentages.
   b. Only water, milk, and eggs may be measured by volume.
   c. The basic units of measure are the United States and metric units.
2. In the metric system:
   a. The gram is the basic unit of weight.
   b. The liter is the basic unit of volume.
   c. The meter is the basic unit of length.
   d. The degree Celsius is the basic unit of temperature.
3. In the metric system:
   a. kilo- = 1,000
   b. deci- = 1/10 or 0.1
   c. centi- = 1/100 or 0.01
   d. milli- = 1/1,000 or 0.001
4. Remember this formula for determining baker's percentages:

$$\frac{\text{total weight of ingredient}}{\text{total weight of flour}} \times 100\% = \text{percent of ingredient}$$

5. Bakers control gluten by adjusting a number of factors.
   a. Type of flour
   b. Shortening
   c. Liquid
   d. Mixing

6. The seven steps of the baking process are:
    a. Formation and expansion of gases
    b. Trapping of gases in air cells
    c. Gelatinization of starches
    d. Coagulation of proteins
    e. Evaporation of some water
    f. Melting of shortenings
    g. Crust formation and browning
7. Staling occurs when baked goods lose moisture and undergo chemical changes in the starch structure.
    a. Staling can be minimized using these three methods:
        (1) Protecting the product from air
        (2) Adding moisture retainers to the formula
        (3) Freezing

Chapter 2

1. Flour is the paramount ingredient in the bakeshop.
2. The four basic types of hard wheat flour are:
    a. Straight
    b. Patent
    c. Clear
    d. High-gluten
3. The three basic types of soft wheat flour are:
    a. Bread
    b. Cake
    c. Pastry
4. The miscellaneous flours are:
    a. All-purpose
    b. Self-rising
    c. Whole wheat
    d. Bran

5. The types of rye flour are:
   a. Light rye
   b. Medium rye
   c. Dark rye
   d. Rye meal (pumpernickel flour)
   e. Rye blend
6. Starches used in baking include:
   a. Cornstarch
   b. Waxy maize
   c. Instant starches
7. Sugars:
   a. Add sweetness and flavor
   b. Create tenderness and fineness of texture
   c. Give crust color
   d. Increase keeping qualities by retaining moisture
   e. Act as creaming agents with fats and as foaming agents with eggs
   f. Provide food for yeast
8. Know the characteristics of:
   a. Granulated sugar
   b. Confectioners' (powdered) sugar
   c. Dehydrated fondant
   d. Brown sugar
   e. Molasses
   f. Corn syrup
   g. Glucose syrup
   h. Honey
   i. Malt syrup

9. The basic types of fat are:
   a. Shortening
      - Regular
      - Emulsified
   b. Butter
   c. Margarine
      - Cake/baker's
      - Pastry
   d. Oil
   e. Lard
10. The basic types of milk products are:
    a. Fresh liquid milk
       - Whole
       - Skim and nonfat
    b. Cream
       - Whipping
       - Light
       - Half-and-half
    c. Fermented milk products
       - Buttermilk
       - Sour cream
       - Yogurt
    d. Evaporated and condensed milk
    e. Dried milk
       - Dried whole
       - Nonfat dry
       - Cheese
       - Baker's
       - Cream

11. Egg types are:
    a. Fresh (shell)
    b. Frozen
    c. Dried
12. Eggs add the following to baked goods:
    a. Emulsifiers of fats and liquids
    b. Leavening
    c. Shortening
    d. Moisture
    e. Flavor
    f. Nutritional value
    g. Color
13. Yeast is discussed on text pages 36–38.
14. The three types of chemical leaveners are:
    a. Baking soda
    b. Baking powder
    c. Baking ammonia
15. Air and steam also act as leaveners.
16. Gelatin is a water-soluble protein used to add strength to baked goods.
17. Know the nuts and nut products commonly used in baking.
18. Know the characteristics of the following chocolate and cocoa products:
    a. Cocoa
    b. Bitter chocolate
    c. Sweet chocolate
    d. Milk chocolate
    e. Cocoa butter
    f. White chocolate
19. Salt enhances flavor, strengthens, enhances the pliability of gluten, and controls fermentation.
20. Spices are derived from vegetable and plant seeds, flower buds, roots, and bark.
21. Vanilla and vanilla extract are used in both baked and unbaked goods.

22. Extracts are flavorful oils dissolved in alcohol.

23. Emulsions are flavorful oils mixed with water and emulsifiers.

24. Alcohols, especially liqueurs and wines, are used to flavor baked goods.

Chapter 3

1. There are three types of yeast products: lean, rich, and rolled-in.

2. Lean dough products are low in fat and sugar.

3. Rich dough products have higher proportions of fat and sugar, and sometimes eggs.

4. Rolled-in yeast dough products layer fat and dough through a rolling and folding technique.

5. There are twelve basic steps in the yeast bread production process; you should know the characteristics of each.
   a. Scaling ingredients
   b. Mixing
      - Straight dough
      - Modified straight dough
      - Sponge
   c. Fermentation
   d. Punching
   e. Scaling
   f. Rounding
   g. Benching
   h. Makeup and panning
   i Proofing
   j. Baking
   k. Cooling
   l. Storing

6. There are three principal dough-mixing methods: the straight dough method, the modified straight dough method, and the sponge method. Know the characteristics, advantages, and disadvantages of each.

7. Three types of washes are used to brush yeast products just before baking:
    a. Water
    b. Starch paste
    c. Egg wash
8. Loaves often are cut or scored (or docked) to allow expansion.
9. Sourdough breads contain a sour, a sponge that is allowed to ferment.
10. Bakers control fermentation by controlling time, temperature, and yeast quantity.
11. Retarding slows the fermentation or proof of yeast.
12. Review the common bread faults and their causes on page 62.

Chapter 4

1. Know the characteristics and special production techniques for the following types of yeast breads:
    a. Crisp-crusted
    b. Soft-crusted
    c. Sourdough
    d. Specialty breads
2. Know the makeup techniques for the following:
    a. Crisp-crusted and rye products
    b. Soft rolls, pan loaves, and braided breads

Chapter 5

1. Review the formulas for preparing sweet and rich doughs.
2. The rolled-in dough formula is used to make croissant dough (also called Danish pastry dough, croissant-style) and Danish dough, brioche-style.
3. Many different fillings and toppings are used to make sweet pastries, including cinnamon sugar, crumb topping, and clear glaze.

Chapter 6

1. Know the techniques for the three basic mixing methods for quick breads:
   a. Biscuit method
   b. Muffin method
   c. Creaming method

Chapter 7

1. Yeast-raised doughnuts are prepared using the modified straight dough method.
2. Cake-type doughnuts are typically prepared using large-scale equipment.
3. Properly fried doughnuts absorb about 2 ounces of fat per dozen.
4. Know the considerations for properly caring for frying fat, discussed on text page 155.
5. French doughnuts are made from éclair paste.
6. Know the formulas, mixing, and preparation techniques for pancake and waffle varieties.
7. American-style pancakes and waffles are made from pourable batters mixed by the muffin method.
8. Know the differences between pancake and waffle batters.
9. Crêpes are thin, unleavened pancakes.
10. Know the various crêpe varieties described on text page 168.

Chapter 8

1. Syrup strength and hardness depend on the temperature to which it is cooked.
2. Graininess results when sugar crystallizes instead of staying dissolved in the syrup.
3. Two basic syrups are simple syrup or stock syrup, and dessert syrup.
4. Know the characteristics of basic creams: whipped cream, meringue, crème anglaise, pastry cream, and chocolate creams.

5. Review the five basic types of dessert sauce:
   a. Custard
   b. Chocolate
   c. Lemon
   d. Fruit
   e. Caramel

Chapter 9

1. Common ingredients of pie doughs include:
   a. Flour
   b. Fat
   c. Liquid
   d. Salt
2. There are two basic types of pie dough:
   a. Flaky pie dough cuts the fat into the flour but does not achieve a uniform mixture and is typically used for top crusts.
   b. Mealy pie dough completely blends the fat and flour and is typically used for bottom crusts because it resists saturation.
3. Know the techniques for preparing baked and unbaked pies.
4. Review common causes and cures for soggy pie bottoms.
5. Several starches typically are used in pie fillings:
   a. Cornstarch
   b. Waxy maize
   c. Modified starches
   d. Flour
   e. Tapioca
   f. Potato starch
   g. Rice starch
   h. Instant (pregelatinized) starch
6. Fruit pie fillings are pieces of solid fruit bound by a gel. Fillings may be prepared from fresh, frozen, canned, or dried fruits.

7. Three methods are used for fruit pies:
    a. Cooked juice method
    b. Cooked fruit method
    c. Old-fashioned method
8. Know the methods used to prepare soft-filling pies such as custard, pumpkin, and pecan.
9. Cream pie fillings are the same as puddings.
10. Chiffon pies are thickened with one of the following:
    a. Starch
    b. Egg
    c. Starch and egg
11. Know the common pie faults and their causes on text page 226.

Chapter 10

1. Pâte brisée is mixed like pie dough and often used to make large tarts.
2. Other pâte-type doughs are mixed using the creaming method.
3. Puff pastry is a rolled-in dough.
    a. Butter is the preferred fat for puff pastry.
    b. Puff pastry dough can consist of more than 1,000 layers of dough and fat.
    c. Other puff-type pastry doughs are blitz puff pastry and reversed puff pastry.
4. Éclair paste, or choux paste, is used to make éclairs and cream puffs.
    a. Know the method for making éclair paste, described on text page 247.
5. Strudel and phyllo doughs start with paper-thin layers of dough that are brushed with fat, then stacked or rolled up.
6. Meringues are often bagged out into shapes and baked until they are crisp, and sometimes used as bases for a variety of pastries.

Chapter 11

1. Unlike pie pans, tart pans are shallow and straight-sided.
2. Simple tarts consist of unbaked tart shells filled with a layer of fresh fruit and sugar.
3. Know the characteristics of the French pastries described in Chapter 11.

Chapter 12

1. The three main goals of cake mixing are to:
    a. Combine ingredients into a smooth, uniform mixture.
    b. Form and incorporate air cells.
    c. Develop the proper texture.
2. The following factors can cause curdling:
    a. Using the wrong type of fat
    b. Using ingredients that are too cold
    c. Mixing the first stage too quickly
    d. Adding liquids too quickly
    e. Adding too much liquid
3. High-fat or shortened cakes are mixed using one of three methods:
    a. Creaming
        -   Used for butter cakes
    b. Two-stage
        -   Used for high-ratio cakes
        -   Liquids are added in stages
    c. Flour-batter
        -   Used for a few specialty items
4. Low-fat or egg-foam cakes, leavened by air trapped in beaten eggs, are mixed using one of three methods:
    a. Sponge (begin with whole-egg or egg-yolk foams)
    b. Angel food
        -   Begin with egg-white foams
        -   Contains no fat
        -   Dry ingredients folded into egg whites
    c. Chiffon
        -   Begin with egg-white foams
        -   Flour, egg yolk, oil, and water batter folded into egg whites
5. A few European-style cakes are prepared using a combination creaming/sponge mixing method.

6. Balancing cake formulas depends upon a knowledge of ingredient functions and of basic principles for each type of cake.

7. Know the scaling, panning, and baking procedures described on text pages 303–306.

8. Cake formulas must be adjusted for changes in altitude.

Chapter 13

1. There are seven basic types of icing:
    a. Fondant
    b. Buttercream
    c. Foam-type
    d. Fudge-type
    e. Flat
    f. Royal or decorator's
    g. Glazes

2. Fondant is a sugar syrup that is crystallized to a smooth, creamy white mass.

3. There are six varieties of buttercream:
    a. Simple
    b. Decorator's
    c. Meringue-type
    d. French
    e   Pastry cream-type
    f. Fondant-type

4. Buttercreams often are mixed with flavorings such as chocolate, coffee, or almond paste.

5. Three types of foam-type icing include:
    a. Plain boiled
    b. Marshmallow
    c. Chocolate foam

6. Fudge-type icings are rich and heavy.

7. Royal icing is similar to flat icings except that it is thicker and made with egg whites.

8. Simple American-style cakes include cupcakes, sheet cakes, and layer cakes.

9. Specialty cakes include:

    a. Boston cream pie

    b. Cake rolls

    c. Ice cream cakes

    d. French pastry

10. Know the tools for cake decorating described on text pages 349–350.

11. There are two methods for decorating cakes with a pastry bag:

    a. Contact method

    b. Falling method

12. Other techniques for decorating cakes include:

    a. Masking the sides

    b. Stenciling

    c. Marbling

    d. Palette knife patterns

    e. Piping jelly

    f. Adding fruits, nuts, or other items

Chapter 14

1. Many European-style cakes are referred to as *gâteaux* (the French word for *cake*) and *tortes* (the German word for *layered cake*).

2. Sometimes a soft filling or mousse, such as Bavarian cream, is used to fill in a layer cake.

3. Marzipan, a paste made of almonds and sugar, is sometimes used to coat cakes.

Chapter 15

1. Know the four cookie characteristics and the factors that contribute to them:

    a. Crispness

    b. Softness

    c. Chewiness

    d. Spread

2. The three cookie mixing methods are:

   a. One-stage

   b. Creaming

   c. Sponge

3. The eight cookie makeup methods are:

   a. Bagged

   b. Dropped

   c. Rolled

   d. Molded

   e. Icebox

   f. Bar

   g. Sheet

   h. Stencil

4. Know the techniques for panning, baking, and cooling cookies described on text pages 400–401.

5. Know the different petits fours secs, or dry cookie-like pastries, described on text page 402.

Chapter 16

1. There are two types of custard:

   a. Stirred

   b. Baked

2. There are three types of rangetop pudding:

   a. Cornstarch pudding (blancmange)

   b. Creamed

   c. Puddings bound with gelatin

3. Baked puddings are custards that contain additional ingredients.

4. Steamed puddings are heavy and dense and best served in cold weather.

5. Bavarians, or Bavarian creams, are made from custard sauce (crème anglaise), gelatin, and whipped cream.

6. Mousses are any soft or creamy dessert made fluffy with whipped cream, beaten egg whites, or both.
7. Soufflés are lightened with beaten egg whites and baked. They contain three elements:
   a. Base
   b. Flavorings
   c. Egg whites

Chapter 17

1. Churn-frozen desserts are mixed constantly during freezing to keep ice crystals small and to incorporate air.
2. Know the factors that contribute to the smoothness, overrun, and mouth feel of churn-frozen desserts.
3. Popular ice cream desserts include parfaits and sundaes (coupes).
4. Still-frozen desserts are frozen in a container without mixing them. They include:
   a. Bombes
   b   Frozen soufflés
   c. Frozen mousses
5. Know the techniques for preparing parfaits, bombes, frozen mousses, and frozen soufflés described on text pages 473–482.

Chapter 18

1. Know the characteristics of and factors in choosing the fruits described on text pages 486–489.
2. Traditional fruit desserts include:
   a. Cobbler
   b. Crisp
   c. Betty
   d. Compote
   e. Sautéed fruit

Chapter 19

1. There are two basic types of dessert presentations:
   a. Simple presentations
   b. Complex presentations
2. Simple presentations feature a single dessert portion served in one of four ways:
   a. Alone
   b. With garnish
   c. With sauce
   d. With garnish and sauce
3. Complex presentations feature two or more dessert portions served alone or with any combination of garnishes and sauces.

Chapter 20

1. In addition to flavoring, chocolate is used for decorative work.
2. The steps in the tempering process are:
   a. Melting
   b. Tempering
   c. Rewarming
3. Tempered chocolate has a variety of decorative uses.
   a. Cutouts
   b. Strips and fans
   c. Cigarettes and curls
   d. Piping
   e. Modeling
   f. Spraying
   g. Dipping
   h. Molding

Chapter 21

1. Marzipan is a paste made of almonds and sugar and can be rolled or modeled.
2. Know the techniques for forming shapes with marzipan described on text pages 553–555.
3. Pastillage is a sugar paste used for modeling.
   a. Pastillage dries quickly and unused portions should be kept covered while working with it.
4. Nougatine is a candy made of caramelized sugar and almonds.

Chapter 22

1. Know the characteristics of boiled syrups described on text pages 566–567.
2. Spun sugar is a mass of sugar strands used to decorate cakes and showpieces.
3. Poured sugar is boiled sugar that is allowed to harden into various shapes.
4. Pulled sugar refers to manipulating sugar to form shapes.
5. Sugar is blown in much the same way as glass.

Practice Test

This Practice Test contains 80 multiple-choice questions that are similar in content and format to those found on The Educational Foundation's final examination for this course. Mark the best answer to each question by circling the appropriate letter. Answers to the Practice Test are on page 91 of this Student Workbook.

Lesson 1: Introduction to Professional Baking

1. Which of the following ingredients is most appropriate to measure by volume?
   A. Flour
   B. Sugar
   C. Milk
   D. Salt

2. Which of the following is 1,000 grams?
   A. Centigram
   B. Kilogram
   C. Decigram
   D. Milligram

3. In baker's percentages, what ingredient is always 100 percent?
   A. Water
   B. Butter
   C. Eggs
   D. Flour

4. The classification of flour as being strong or weak is determined by the flour's
   A. bleaching process.
   B. protein content.
   C. age.
   D. flavor.

5. The three gases primarily responsible for the leavening of baked goods are air, steam, and
   A. helium.
   B. carbon monoxide.
   C. carbon dioxide.
   D. nitrous oxide.

6. Which term describes the process by which gluten absorbs moisture and becomes firmer?
   A. Staling
   B. Kneading
   C. Gelatinization
   D. Coagulation

7. Which of the following ingredients increases a baked product's browning?
   A. Flour
   B. Baking powder
   C. Eggs
   D. Baking soda

8. Which ingredient acts as a moisture retainer and, thus, can reduce staling?

    A. Baking powder
    B. Butter
    C. Flour
    D. Vanilla

9. Which ingredient tenderizes, retains moisture, gives crust color, and "feeds" yeast?

    A. Flour
    B. Shortening
    C. Sugar
    D. Egg

10. Which type of sugar is created from the byproducts of a sucrose solution heated with an acid?

    A. Table
    B. Brown
    C. Invert
    D. Confectioners'

11. When substituting buttermilk for regular milk, what must you add to the buttermilk to neutralize its acidity?

    A. Molasses
    B. Baking powder
    C. Baking soda
    D. Cream of tartar

12. Which ingredient accounts for at least half the ingredient cost of an average cake batter?

    A. Egg
    B. Flour
    C. Sugar
    D. Shortening

13. Which leavening agent's reactivity depends on the presence of acid ingredients in the formula?

    A. Yeast
    B. Baking soda
    C. Baking powder
    D. Baking ammonia

Lesson 2: Yeast Doughs

14. Which type of dough products tend to be flaky?

    A. Rich
    B. Lean
    C. Folded-in
    D. Rolled-in

15. Which yeast product is made with lean dough?

    A. Brioche
    B. Pizza crust
    C. Sweet rolls
    D. Danish pastry

16. Which of the following indicates
that the fermentation of yeast dough
is complete?
   A. Dent remains in dough when
      pressed lightly
   B. Dough temperature reaches
      80°F (27°C)
   C. Crust forms on dough
   D. Dough falls in on itself

17. Proofing is a continuation of which
earlier yeast production step?
   A. Punching
   B. Rounding
   C. Panning
   D. Fermentation

18. Which yeast bread production step is
omitted for hearth breads?
   A. Panning
   B. Rounding
   C. Scaling
   D. Proofing

19. Which wash typically is used for
rye products?
   A. Egg
   B. Water
   C. Starch paste
   D. Milk

20. For which type of bread dough is
commercial yeast an optional
ingredient?
   A. Sourdoughs
   B. Sponge doughs
   C. Short-fermentation straight doughs
   D. Long-fermentation straight doughs

21. Which yeast bread products are boiled
in a malt solution before being baked?
   A. English muffins
   B. Croissants
   C. Hard rolls
   D. Bagels

22. What equipment is used to make
English muffins and crumpets?
   A. Deep-fat fryer
   B. Double boiler
   C. Steamer
   D. Griddle

23. Which of the following ingredients
makes rich doughs tender?
   A. Liquid
   B. Sour
   C. Patent flour
   D. Fat and eggs

24. Which ingredient contributes most to
the flaky texture of rolled-in dough
products?
   A. Yeast
   B. Sugar
   C. Fat
   D. Eggs

Lesson 3: Quick Breads, Doughnuts, Basic Sauces, and Pies

25. The muffin method is characterized by
    A. thorough mixing.
    B. quickness and ease.
    C. light kneading.
    D. prebaking proofing.

26. Which technique produces softer biscuits without crusty sides?
    A. Brushing with egg wash or milk
    B. Lining sheets with silicone paper
    C. Twisting the hand cutter while cutting biscuits
    D. Baking biscuits with sides touching

27. When is a batter mixed enough when using the muffin method?
    A. When the dry ingredients are moistened
    B. When it runs off the end of a spoon
    C. When it sticks to a fork
    D. When it forms streaks on the side of the mixing bowl

28. Yeast-raised doughnut dough is most like which yeast bread formula?
    A. Sourdough
    B. Brioche
    C. Danish pastry dough
    D. Regular sweet dough

29. What is a typical average fat temperature for frying doughnuts?
    A. 285°F
    B. 325°F
    C. 375°F
    D. 435°F

30. What is the primary disadvantage of using solid shortening to fry doughnuts?
    A. Instability
    B. Higher cost
    C. Failure to congeal when cooled
    D. Unpleasant eating quality

31. Which ingredient is sometimes added to the 4X sugar used to powder doughnuts?
    A. Flour
    B. Cream of tartar
    C. Coconut
    D. Cornstarch

32. What is used to make French doughnuts?
    A. Bavarian cream
    B. Éclair paste
    C. Coulis
    D. Praline

33. Batters leavened with which of the following can be made the night before and stored in the cooler until needed the next day?
    A. Baking powder only
    B. Baking soda only
    C. Baking powder and beaten egg whites
    D. Baking soda plus baking powder

34. Orange, lemon, liqueur, and cognac are key ingredients in which crêpe dessert?
    A. Crêpes Normande
    B. Crêpes Frangipane
    C. Crêpes Suzette
    D. Glazed crêpes

35. Inversion is employed to prevent which of the following in a syrup?
    A. Thinning
    B. Crystallization
    C. Thickening
    D. Browning

36. Cream for whipping should be
    A. very fresh.
    B. cold.
    C. tempered.
    D. scalded.

37. What is the key ingredient of meringue?
    A. Cream
    B. Buttermilk
    C. Simple syrup
    D. Egg whites

38. Which of the following stabilizes meringue?
    A. Butter
    B. Sugar
    C. Water
    D. Flour

39. Vanilla custard is also known as
    A. crème anglaise.
    B. ganache.
    C. fondant.
    D. Italian meringue.

40. Chocolate cream is also known as
    A. crème anglaise.
    B. ganache.
    C. fondant.
    D. Italian meringue.

41. Which of the following is most likely to toughen pie dough?
    A. Salt
    B. Shortening
    C. Excess liquid
    D. Low temperatures

42. Which pie dough requires that the fat remain in pieces the size of walnuts?
    A. Long-flake
    B. Short-flake
    C. Short dough
    D. Mealy dough

43. Which type of dough should be used for pie bottoms?
    A. Long-flake
    B. Short-flake
    C. Lattice
    D. Mealy

Lesson 4: Pastries, Tarts, and Cakes

44. What is the preferred fat to use in puff pastry?
    A. Shortening
    B. Butter
    C. Lard
    D. Margarine

45. Why is it important for tart dough to be flavorful?
    A. Less filling is used than for pies.
    B. More fat is used than for pies.
    C. Less sugar is used than for pies.
    D. More baking powder is used than for pies.

46. Air cells in a cake batter are formed during which stage?
    A. Panning
    B. Mixing
    C. Baking
    D. Sifting

47. Which type of cake contains no fat?
    A. Chiffon
    B. Sponge
    C. Angel food
    D. Two-stage

48. The fundamental ingredient for all types of sponge cake is
    A. butter and sugar emulsion.
    B. high-ratio shortening and flour emulsion.
    C. an egg foam containing yolks.
    D. an egg white foam.

49. Why should shortening not be substituted for butter in equal measure?
    A. Shortening contains more fat.
    B. Shortening is more flavorful.
    C. Shortening contains more water.
    D. Shortening mixes more smoothly.

50. When a toothpick inserted into a baked cake comes out clean it means that the cake
    A. contains too much fat.
    B. is underdone.
    C. contains too much liquid.
    D. is done.

51. When baking cakes at high altitudes, which of the following must be decreased?
    A. Liquid
    B. Egg
    C. Shortening
    D. Flour

52. What ingredient amount is different in chocolate cakes than in devil's food cakes?
    A. Baking powder
    B. Baking soda
    C. Flour
    D. Cocoa

53. Which of the following is a sugar syrup crystallized to a smooth, creamy white mass?
    A. Royal icing
    B. Flat icing
    C. Gelatin-based glaze
    D. Fondant

54. When used to ice pastries and cakes, buttercream should be
    A. at room temperature.
    B. warm.
    C. cool.
    D. cold.

55. Marshmallow icing is a
    A. foam-type icing.
    B. fondant.
    C. glaze.
    D. flat icing.

56. Which icing works best for marbling a cake?
    A. Royal icing
    B. Buttercream
    C. Flat icing
    D. Fondant

57. Gâteaux and tortes are types of
    A. tart.
    B. éclair.
    C. cake.
    D. pie.

58. Marzipan is used for which part of a European-style cake?
    A. Coating
    B. Filling
    C. Bottom layer
    D. Specialty layer

59. Which technique do bakers use to ice a cake completely with fondant?
    A. Pouring
    B. Spreading
    C. Pastry bag
    D. Paper cone

Lesson 5: Cookies, Custards, Frozen Desserts, and Fruit Desserts

60. Increasing both sugar and fat will increase a cookie's
    A. crispness.
    B. softness.
    C. chewiness.
    D. spread.

61. Which of the following will increase cookies' spread?
    A. Decreasing liquid in the batter
    B. Decreasing the amount of sugar used
    C. Higher baking temperatures
    D. Using heavily greased pans

62. Italian biscotti are examples of which type of cookie?
    A. Sheet
    B. Bar
    C. Icebox
    D. Dropped

63. Ungreased pans are best to use with cookies containing a large amount of
    A. fat.
    B. flour.
    C. sugar.
    D. spread.

64. Which is the most effective way to avoid burnt bottoms on rich dough cookies?
    A. Double-pan the cookies
    B. Cool on baking sheets
    C. Raise temperature and reduce baking time
    D. Bake on greased and floured pans

65. Which of the following may cause cookies to crack?
    A. Storing before completely cool
    B. Cooling on cookie sheets
    C. Cooling too rapidly in cold drafts
    D. Cooling on silicone paper

66. Cream puddings differ from pastry cream in that cream puddings
    A. contain eggs.
    B. contain less starch.
    C. are boiled, not baked.
    D. contain less sugar.

67. Which of the following typically are very heavy?
    A. Range-top puddings
    B. Gelatin puddings
    C. Steamed puddings
    D. Baked puddings

68. Which of the following desserts contains a gelatin base?
    A. Mousse
    B. Bavarian
    C. Steamed pudding
    D. Baked pudding

69. Folding egg whites into a hot base will do which of the following to a mousse?

    A. Make it deflate
    B. Make it more stable
    C. Make it run
    D. Make it form a skin

70. Blancmange is thickened with

    A. flour.
    B. bread.
    C. cornstarch.
    D. eggs.

71. What additional ingredient is included in French-style ice cream?

    A. Egg yolks
    B. Vanilla bean
    C. Egg whites
    D. Honey

72. "Overrun" refers to incorporation of which of the following in ice cream?

    A. Ice crystals
    B. Milk or cream
    C. Water
    D. Air

73. Which type of dessert consists of a molded ice cream or sherbet coating filled with a compatibly flavored frozen mixture?

    A. Frozen soufflé
    B. Frozen mousse
    C. Coupe
    D. Bombe

74. Regardless of the bases into which it is mixed, which ingredient gives all frozen mousses their light texture?

    A. Whipped egg white
    B. Whipped cream
    C. Egg yolk foam
    D. Gelatin

75. Which fruit dessert is most similar to a two-crust pie without the bottom crust?

    A. Cobbler
    B. Betty
    C. Compote
    D. Crisp

Lesson 6: Decoration and Presentation

76. Which of the following exemplifies a complex dessert presentation?

    A. A dessert plus garnish and a sauce.
    B. An elegant pastry served on a plate with an attractive design.
    C. A frozen dessert topped with whipped cream and chocolate curls and accompanied by a petit four sec.
    D. Two or more desserts on one plate.

77. Which heat source is best to use for melting chocolate?

    A. Stovetop
    B. Microwave oven
    C. Slow oven
    D. Hot water

78. For best results, which type of bowl should be used for mixing marzipan and pastillage?

    A. Aluminum
    B. Glass
    C. Stainless steel
    D. Plastic

79. Cornstarch, royal icing, and sandpaper are used in producing decorative work made from

    A. marzipan.
    B. pastillage.
    C. nougat.
    D. boiled sugar.

80. "Pearling" refers to

    A. cooling blown sugar.
    B. blowing syrup into shapes.
    C. the color of spun sugar.
    D. pulling and folding pulled sugar.

Practice Test Answers and Text Page References

1. C . . . . p. 5	28. D . . . . p. 154	55. A . . . . p. 340
2. B . . . . p. 8	29. C . . . . p. 154	56. D . . . . p. 356
3. D . . . . p. 10	30. D . . . . p. 155	57. C . . . . p. 362
4. B . . . . p. 12	31. D . . . . p. 158	58. A . . . . p. 363
5. C . . . . p. 13	32. B . . . . p. 159	59. A . . . . p. 368
6. D . . . . p. 12	33. A . . . . p. 164	60. A . . . . p. 394
7. C . . . . p. 14	34. C . . . . p. 168	61. D . . . . p. 395
8. B . . . . p. 15	35. B . . . . p. 176	62. B . . . . p. 399
9. C . . . . p. 23	36. B . . . . p. 180	63. A . . . . p. 400
10. C . . . . p. 23	37. D . . . . p. 181	64. A . . . . p. 400
11. C . . . . p. 32	38. B . . . . p. 183	65. C . . . . p. 401
12. A . . . . p. 33	39. A . . . . p. 184	66. B . . . . p. 429
13. B . . . . p. 37	40. B . . . . p. 192	67. C . . . . p. 437
14. D . . . . p. 50	41. C . . . . p. 202	68. B . . . . p. 439
15. B . . . . p. 50	42. A . . . . p. 203	69. B . . . . p. 440
16. A . . . . p. 53	43. D . . . . p. 203	70. C . . . . p. 428
17. D . . . . p. 55	44. B . . . . p. 233	71. A . . . . p. 462
18. A . . . . p. 56	45. A . . . . pp. 230, 268	72. D . . . . p. 463
19. C . . . . p. 56	46. B . . . . p. 292	73. D . . . . p. 473
20. A . . . . p. 58	47. C . . . . p. 299	74. B . . . . p. 477
21. D . . . . p. 85	48. C . . . . p. 297	75. A . . . . p. 490
22. D . . . . p. 85	49. A . . . . p. 295	76. D . . . . p. 512
23. D . . . . p. 106	50. D . . . . p. 306	77. D . . . . p. 535
24. C . . . . p. 112	51. C . . . . p. 308	78. C . . . . pp. 552, 556
25. B . . . . p. 136	52. B . . . . p. 309	79. B . . . . pp. 556–557
26. D . . . . p. 138	53. D . . . . p. 334	80. D . . . . p. 573
27. A . . . . p. 136	54. A . . . . p. 335	